To:

_____

From:

_____

On the occasion of the

Thanksgiving Celebration

Thursday, **N**ovember _____

THE
Thanksgiving
Ceremony

THE
Thanksgiving
Ceremony

NEW

TRADITIONS for

AMERICA'S

FAMILY FEAST

EDWARD BLEIER

Foreword by WILLIAM SAFIRE

Illustrations by Dorothy Reinhardt

 Crown Publishers New York

Published by Crown Publishers, New York, New York.
Member of the Crown Publishing Group, a division of Random House, Inc. www.randomhouse.com

CROWN is a trademark and the Crown colophon is a registered trademark of Random House, Inc.

Please see page 125 for acknowledgment of permission to print from previously published material.

All Crown titles are available at a discount when purchasing in quantity for sales promotions or corporate use. Special editions, including personalized covers, excerpts and corporate imprints can be created when purchasing in large quantities. For more information, please call Premium Sales at (800) 800-3246 or email specialmarkets@randomhouse.com.

Printed in the United States of America

Design by Karen Minster

Library of Congress Cataloging-in-Publication Data
Bleier, Edward.
   The Thanksgiving ceremony : new traditions for
America's family feast / Edward Bleier.—1st ed.
        p.   cm.
   1. Thanksgiving Day. I. Title.
   GT4975.B54 2003
   394.2649—dc21

                                        2003000779

ISBN 1-4000-4787-0

10 9 8 7 6 5 4 3 2 1

First Edition

For my wife, Magda Palacci.
She brought me love and a
wonderful family,
after mine was gone;
and rekindled the gratitude
of yet another generation of
"new" Americans—
for the opportunities of
this great country.

~

CONTENTS

I

The History of Thanksgiving   2 5

II

The Thanksgiving Ceremony   5 1

III

Inspirational Thanksgiving Material 73

~

FOREWORD

By William Safire

 "FOR ALL THE CREATURES OF GOD ARE good," went a 1539 translation of the Bible, "and nothing to be refused, yf it be receaved with thankesgevynge."

That was the first use in English of "thanksgiving" as one word. As the book that follows will inform you, the beautiful locution was taken up by the Pilgrims of the Plymouth colony in 1621 to mark their first year's triumph over privation. The day was capitalized in John Adams's diary in 1760, declared a day to be "set apart" by the Continental Congress in 1777 to mark the victory over General Burgoyne's redcoats at Saratoga, and later proclaimed a holiday by President Washington, once at the beginning and again at the end of his presidency.

Thomas Jefferson, however, with his strong opinion about the separation of church and state, believed that such prayer should spring from the people and not be proclaimed by officialdom. He pointedly refrained from following Washington's precedent, and sure enough, as Jefferson probably hoped, for six

decades the tradition of showing communal gratitude
at the autumnal bounty continued and grew stronger
without a political blessing from the nation's chief
magistrate. When state governors moved into the
proclamation vacuum, they added a note of confusion because the time of harvest differed from North
to South; there were local holidays separated by
weeks, but no "national" Thanksgiving Day.

Then in 1863 came the Civil War's turning point:
The Union scored a pair of decisive victories at
Gettysburg and Vicksburg. William Seward, President Lincoln's onetime rival who had become his sec-
retary of state, drafted a declaration for Lincoln's
signature that—like Congress's earlier proclamation
following Saratoga—commemorated not just the military achievements but the human sacrifice in battles.
"It is meet and right to recognize and confess the presence of the Almighty Father and the power of His
Hand equally in these triumphs and these sorrows,"
wrote Seward for Lincoln. "Now, therefore, be it
known that I do set apart Thursday, the 6th day of
August next, to be observed as a day for National
Thanksgiving, Praise and Prayer."

Lincoln signed it. The man from Illinois, who
rarely attended church, had been criticized often for
his lack of public piety. His was a personal and private religious belief; not long before, another Cabinet

member had to remind him at the last minute to add an uplifting line to his legalistic Emancipation Declaration to include a reference to "Divine Providence."

Why, given the reluctance of the man whom many called Father Abraham to express religious convictions in his official papers, did Lincoln accept the highly reverent draft by Seward? Because, I think, the wartime president wanted to share with those he considered his fellow citizens of the South a search for spiritual comfort to accompany the whole country's grief at the shedding of American blood: "Domestic affliction *in every part of the country,*" he noted sadly, "follows in the train of these fearful bereavements."

That was a special day given over to prayers of thanksgiving; it was not, however, America's first annual Thanksgiving Day. That permanent holiday came about, journalists are happy to point out, through the urging of a woman who called herself an editress. Sarah J. Hale, advocate of education for women, whose *Lady's Book* was for forty years one of the most influential periodicals of its time, crusaded in her magazine and in letters to both Lincoln and Seward "to have the day of our annual Thanksgiving made a National and fixed Union Festival."

This idea made practical political sense. Lincoln (like his Confederate counterpart, Jeff Davis) was having difficulty maintaining authority over some governors. State sovereignty was asserted as the armies of both North and South were recruited and marched proudly under state flags. Needed to rally war-weary citizens was some act of nationalization, a symbolic tightening of the bonds of unity.

Lincoln seized the opportunity presented by the "editress" (a formulation that never caught on) to draw Americans together on both national and religious grounds. In 1864, with his reelection far from certain, he chose to call on "my fellow citizens *wherever they may then be*"—again, which included Americans in the states whose secession Lincoln refused to accept—to observe "a day of Thanksgiving and Praise to Almighty God the beneficent Creator and Ruler of the Universe." The first annual proclamation that Sarah Hale had lobbied for was, according to Lincoln Secretaries Nicolay and Hay, "written by Seward and is in his handwriting." It was unstinting in its religious fervor, urging citizens to "reverently humble themselves in the dust and from thence offer up penitent and fervent prayers and supplications to the Great Disposer of events for a return of the inestimable blessings of Peace, Union and Harmony throughout the land."

The moral purpose of Lincoln's uncharacteristic religiosity was to unify deeply divided Americans around an event already steeped in tradition and reflecting a common spiritual value. His political purpose in nationalizing Thanksgiving Day, making it the same day throughout the country, and "set apart" (evoking the phrase chosen by George Washington) by the nation's president, was to emphasize the symbol of central authority. Both the moral and the political purposes were well served at the time the Union was in peril of being sundered.

Today's Americans in every region no longer turn to Thanksgiving Day to assert our sense of national self, or to express gratitude to those who gave the last full measure of devotion. On the Fourth of July we celebrate our independent unity; on Memorial Day we salute our war dead. While Thanksgiving surely retains its religious overtone—as we show reverence to some power outside ourselves that the lawyerly Seward called "the Great Disposer of events"—to many, this uniquely American holiday is not primarily a holy day. Thanksgiving Day does not center on solemn, sectarian religious observance like Christmas or Passover or Ramadan.

As Edward Bleier's timely and wonderfully useful book shows, Thanksgiving is not only a family holiday, but is the holiday of families. The Americans and their guests who come together on the fourth Thursday of November may be related by blood, or by marriage, by friendship, by common interest, or per-

haps just be neighborliness or ethnicity or some combination of all the associations. Although some members of the feast may be bound by habit or driven by
hunger, what brings almost all of us together at a time
of harvest is the longing to be part of a family, real,
virtual, or amalgamated by remarriage. Those unwill-
ing to be thankful to God are at least thankful to be
together and to share a laugh and a slice of turkey on
a day during which nobody should be alone.

On first looking into Bleier's home run, I asked
myself, Where has this book been for all these
Thanksgivings? Getting together for a grand dinner
party may be glorious fun, but a holiday should have
a focus, as most do: a parade and fireworks or a
solemn wreath-laying, a Labor Day labor-free barbe-
cue or a New Year's Eve massing of crowds followed
the next day by an orgy of college bowl games.

Winston Churchill once spurned a dessert with
"Take away this pudding; it has no theme." This long-
overdue book helps us find that focus and develop
that theme, drawing together Thanksgiving Day's history, its hymns and prayers, its poetry and sayings—
all memories-in-the-making that bind the ties of those
at the table and recall those who may be missing but
are not forgotten. The guide to celebration adds the
element of organization in a proposed familial ceremony, giving every guest of any age a chance to par-

ticipate; because the format is adaptable to each gathering's taste, the occasion becomes the creation of those present, more memorable for what is experienced than for what was eaten.

The author-editor and I have been "family" for a half-century, since college days at Syracuse. (We were both dropouts; over a generation later, Ed went back and was graduated.) Even then, working his way through as a student sports broadcaster, Ed had an inkling of the unifying as well as the educational force of the electronic media. That led him to the world of television and motion pictures and through to the "streaming media" on our computers. But as he rose to leadership at Warner Bros. network programming, Bleier became known as one of the most forthright and articulate consciences of an industry too often taken with its own power.

Leading discussions of media ethics and future directions at the Aspen Institute, serving as chairman of the Academy of the Arts of East Hampton's Guild Hall, helping to get the Martha Graham Dance Company on its feet, increasing public awareness and support of brain science as a director of the Dana Foundation—my fraternal friend has given back at least as much the opportunity as he has taken from the country he loves. Because he's "family," in the broadest sense, Bleier is well equipped to help lend inspiring, entertaining, and informative structure to the most familial American holiday.

And so, in a word that has grown in meaning across half a millennium, from my extended family to yours—Happy Thankesgevynge!

INTRODUCTION

 THANKSGIVING HAS ALWAYS BEEN A favorite American holiday. It's a time for good food and good company. A re-dedication of spirit. And fun.

For generations, families and friends have gathered on the fourth Thursday of November to share a banquet and to give thanks for our many bounties. But aside from football and turkey, I've always hungered, certainly not for more food, but for even more "spirit" and ritual.

Thanksgiving was very important to me as a kid. My mother was an immigrant, about nine years old, when her mother and four siblings followed my grandfather from the part of Russia that is now Ukraine. The story of their lives paralleled *Fiddler on the Roof*—to overcome poverty and discrimination, they emigrated to America, "the Golden Land."

My father was the fourth of ten siblings, only six of whom survived their second year. The son of Austrian immigrants, he was the first born in America.

Our Thanksgiving celebrations were especially

poignant. My parents had gone from peasant penury to middle class, and so the bounty of food on our Thanksgiving table was always a wonderment to members of my family.

My mother was an excellent cook and she especially enjoyed preparing a grand meal of a large, succulent turkey, savory stuffing, sweet potato with marshmallow, a variety of overcooked vegetables, and great soups and pies that varied from year to year—altogether a sumptuous feast.

It was also an occasion when aunts, uncles, and cousins would visit, along with neighbors and friends, whose families might not have been intact.

I well remember the Thanksgiving dinners. Our informal proclamations of thanks, our silent prayers, and our spontaneous marvels that America was so welcoming—these were the defining memories, for me, of Thanksgiving.

Of course, my brother and I, as young first-generation American kids, shared the spirit, especially because it was also a long school holiday weekend. But, illness, military duty, more illness, my departure for college, and my mother's death brought an end to our family's Thanksgiving celebrations. Thereafter, my father, brother, and I usually improvised with friends or family—until both of them also passed on.

I was single for a long time, until I married a wonderful European woman and journalist, Magda Palacci, whose family had no tradition of Thanksgiving. They celebrated the Passover Seder and the harvest meals that were traditional in their French and Mediterranean cultures.

Over the years, as my wife and I prepared and celebrated Thanksgiving dinners by ourselves or with our friends, I became fixated on the idea of celebrating in a more formal and meaningful way. For at least twenty-five years I have dreamed about developing a formal ceremony that any family or collection of friends could celebrate during the traditional meal.

The Thanksgiving Ceremony offered here is for families, groups of friends, or a mix of both. It's a ceremony in which participants "go around the table," sometimes reading a portion alone and sometimes reading together in unison. It's a flexible ceremony, and can be performed in any sequence (left to right, youngest to oldest, right to left), and with as much formality as desired. The full ceremony can be completed before the meal, or performed in clusters of readings that are staggered throughout the meal. One person—the host, hostess, or someone the group selects—leads the ceremony.

The material included in the book can be used in various ways, so that families and gatherings of

friends can customize their own Thanksgiving ceremony:

a. The complete Ceremony can be followed as
it is presented here.

b. Additional material—sayings, proclamations,
etc.—is included in the second part for those
who prefer to compose their own ceremony.

c. A third option is to use both the formal
Ceremony and some of the supplementary
material in a combination of your choosing.

The Ceremony has been designed and written to
last for about twenty minutes, so that it can be completed before the meal is served and so those in
charge of cooking and serving can participate without
concern that the food will get cold.

But of course the Ceremony can extend longer if
the group wishes, or be resumed after dinner with the
additional songs, hymns, poems, proclamations, historical passages, toasts, and prayers provided.

So that your guests do not get so hungry as to
rush the Ceremony, I suggest you serve some hors
d'oeuvres before you begin.

By designing this narrative for the Thanksgiving
holiday, I hope to provide continuity from year to
year, and from generation to generation—as well as
continuity across all of America on the Thursday in
November designated as Thanksgiving.

THE
Thanksgiving
Ceremony

The History of
Thanksgiving

WHAT ARE THE FIRST WORDS THAT LEAP TO mind when you think of Thanksgiving?

Probably *the Pilgrims, the* Mayflower, *Plymouth, turkey, the Indians, 1621,* and *football*—though not necessarily in that order. Less likely are *the Vikings; the Spanish; African slaves; 1526; French Protestants; St. Augustine, Florida; New Mexico; the Dutch; the London Company;* and *Jamestown, Virginia.*

The latter all played a role, earlier than the Pilgrims, in the settlement of what was later to become the United States (not to mention 30,000 B.C., the estimated date of America's earliest tribal harvest feasts, many millennia before Columbus stumbled on Western Hemisphere shores).

But traditions have a way of enduring, and the Thanksgiving story we're most familiar with has its roots in the early days of Plymouth Rock, in 1620. To recount this story, we first must start out, as the Pilgrims did, on the other side of the Atlantic. Let's revisit what was happening in England in the sixteenth and early seventeenth centuries.

A key conflict of the time converged on religious issues—between Rome and "reformers." And given the paramount importance of faith in daily life, it was only natural that spiritual allegiance would inform the movement of people and ideas at this seminal juncture in European Colonialism.

So who were these Pilgrims and why did they leave their motherland in Great Britain? After the Protestant Reformation—the epic break from Roman Catholicism that produced the Church of England— protest over religious reforms continued. To some, the Anglican Church was a mirror image of the Vatican, and they called for its purification. These "Puritans" came in greater and lesser shades of zeal, but for the purest of the pure, nothing short of complete and strict fundamentalism was satisfactory.

They were intolerant of many things. For example, they abhorred the "excesses" of the alehouse and the Shakespearean stage. They called for a return to the simplicity of biblical days and an end to the robes and rituals of a "corrupt" clergy. But dissent was a risky business in England. The Separatist cult hardly endeared itself to the Crown, and was soon pushed into hiding or out of the country.

One splinter group had been charting reforms in the Midlands village of Scrooby. When they learned that King James I planned to "harry them from the land," the Scrooby congregation found refuge by crossing the narrow North Sea that separates England from Holland, where they found greater religious tolerance among the Dutch. They fled Amsterdam in 1607–1608 and soon relocated to the coastal town of Leyden, also in the Netherlands. Yet in the gathering war with Catholic Spain, King James once again threatened. England forced its Dutch ally to suppress Separatist life. Taking stock of the growing dangers and hardships of exile in Holland—including the unorthodox pleasures luring Puritan children—a group of Pilgrims began to set their sights on America. They rallied the Virginia Company and London investors in support of their ocean voyage. In July 1620 the first group set sail from Leyden for Southampton, from where they hoped to cross to the New World, and establish a community founded on their own austere religious beliefs.

Four maiden ships brought these "First Comers" to America. The best known, the *Mayflower,* set sail in September 1620. The *Speedwell* was forced to port after springing a leak and never completed its journey. At the English port of Plymouth, some of the *Speedwell*'s passengers were crammed aboard the *Mayflower* to join its original passengers for sixty-five days of seasickness in mostly rough seas. In November 1621 a vessel called the *Fortune* ferried thirty-five more people to

American shores, and in July 1623 the wives and children joined other new colonists aboard the *Anne* and the *Little James*.

Aboard the *Mayflower* were such personalities as Plymouth Colony's first governor, John Carver; William Bradford, its second; and William Brewster, whose Scrooby home had been an early crucible for the Pilgrims. One John Howland made history by cheating death. Plunged overboard in a storm, he held onto a rope until a sailor hauled him back on deck. His descendants include four American presidents: Theodore and Franklin Roosevelt and George H. W. and George W. Bush.

But, of the 102 passengers onboard the *Mayflower,* only about half were Pilgrims, and they came to be known as the Saints. Their co-travelers, the so-called Strangers, were sundry fortune seekers, following earlier émigrés to the British tobacco settlement in Virginia.

Why the ship never made it to Virginia is hotly debated. Some historians believe that the Pilgrim Separatists saw New England as a safer haven from Anglican control because the Crown was already established in Virginia. Others argue that the Dutch, hoping to avoid English settlement in New Amsterdam, coaxed those guiding the *Mayflower* northward with bribes. Still others credit storms and navigational gaffes for the Provincetown Harbor landing. Adding to the suspense are historical rumors of a hijacking plot.

We may never satisfy our curiosity about the reasons, but we do know one thing: When it became clear that anchors would drop well north of Virginia Company turf, conflict broke out aboard the *Mayflower*. The Strangers declared themselves exempt from Pilgrim control. Fearing mutiny, the Pilgrim leaders then drafted an agreement of self-rule. A blueprint for autonomous government, the Mayflower Compact won the endorsement of nearly all the adult men.

Much has been made over this plan for a "civil Body Politick," and justly so. What the *Mayflower* passengers were creating was the precursor for subsequent American governance and constitutional agreements. Every year, it stipulated, the Pilgrims would convene a "General Court to elect the governor and assistants, enact laws, and levy taxes." The Framers of the Constitution clearly took heed and established formal days for elections.

So where did the Pilgrims finally land that November—and what did they know about their destination? This much seems clear: They made landfall at Cape Cod and had maps and guidebooks of New England marking "Plimouth." They were aware of the rich fishing around Cape Cod and had intelligence about the indigenous population who had been ravaged and decimated by diseases borne by earlier visitors from Europe. A number of historians trace the source of information to a Wampanoag Native called Tisquantum, or Squanto.

The Wampanoag belonged to a large confederacy of Algonquin-speaking tribes called the League of the Delaware. For roughly a century these farmers, hunters, and fishermen encountered European explorers whose intentions and power were cause for concern. The traditional custom of the Native tribes was to offer help and hospitality to those in need, yet a growing mistrust of the white intruders—particularly slave merchants who raided indigenous communities and left illness in their wake—discouraged the Natives from their traditional practices. By 1620, the Wampanoag nation had dwindled to fewer than two thousand from some twelve thousand only two decades before.

A pivotal character in the unfolding colonial drama, Squanto possessed vital skills, including fluency in English, that secured his place in history. The historic speculation is that in 1605, fifteen years before the arrival of the Pilgrims, Squanto journeyed to and from England with a British explorer, Captain John Weymouth, who all but adopted him as a son. Squanto was later taken captive by a British slaver and spirited off to the Caribbean Islands.

Squanto's odyssey is the stuff of legends. Highlights include escaping Spain and finding his way back to England and Captain Weymouth, who then paid for his voyage back to America. Among his various Atlantic crossings, possibly totaling six, Squanto docked at what was to become Maine, Newfoundland, and his native Massachusetts.

From his final landing in Massachusetts, he reportedly trekked by foot to his boyhood village of Patuxet, where he found skeletons strewn everywhere. As in so many other Indian communities, disease had ravaged the village. Squanto and a sachem, or chief, named Samoset—another English speaker who had joined him on the return voyage from England—went to live with a neighboring Wampanoag tribe at Pokanoket, home of the nation's Grand Sachem, Massasoit. Empty Patuxet was up for grabs.

When the Pilgrims arrived there, they found the site ready to inhabit: cleared fields, planted corn, a fresh-water brook, and a harbor. Their search for a home in the New World was over. They gave their new habitat a new name: Plymouth. The newcomers not only benefited from the village's stocked provisions but they also enjoyed the assistance of its sole survivor, Squanto, who was dispatched by the great king Massasoit as translator, scout, and go-between.

With Squanto's help, the colonists learned where to

fish and find goods as well as how to plant corn, pumpkins, and squash. Without Squanto's expertise and generosity, they may never have weathered the first New England winter. In his famous journal, Governor Bradford referred to this ordeal as the "Starving Time." The wheat the Europeans had brought with them would not take to the rocky coastal soil, and their earth-covered shelters were no match for the cold.

During Squanto's several months as Bradford's houseguest, he taught the Pilgrims how to build round-roofed houses, or wigwams, from birch bark and elm. Squanto also shared with the Pilgrims medicinal plants plus venison and beaver skins to keep them warm. He showed them how to tap trees for maple sugar, turn fish into fertilizer, and dig and cook clams.

Squanto would stay in Plymouth Colony until succumbing to Indian fever in 1622. He embraced the Pilgrims as the brethren of his beloved English friend, John Weymouth, though his motives may not have been purely altruistic. His power intrigues, including a scheme to topple Massasoit, eventually branded him as traitor to the Wampanoag incumbent. Indeed, Squanto became a source of friction between the two cultures. Yet having made himself indispensable to the Pilgrims, he had powerful friends and protectors.

Bradford regarded Squanto as a divine emissary sent to show the Pilgrims their way in the wilderness.

To the Puritans, the Indians were heathens, and as such, Satan's children. But Squanto was different. As the only baptized Wampanoag (and an educated Christian to boot), he stood as proof that God was on the side of the Pilgrims, His Chosen People.

The Europeans regarded the diseases that destroyed the native populations as further evidence of their chosen status—a divine intervention that proved their primacy in the land. During their first winter, half of the Pilgrims died of scurvy, pneumonia, and other diseases. But the indigenous population had no prior exposure to the likes of smallpox, chicken pox, plague, measles, and influenza, and therefore no immunity. Germs wiped out entire Indian villages. John Winthrop, governor of the Massachusetts Bay Colony, interpreted the pandemic as "miraculous."

Had plague not destroyed the Wampanoag, Massasoit might have greeted the European settlers less openly. But he, like his tribesmen, saw the carnage as punishment from the angered gods and this sapped his will to resist. With his ranks so desperately thinned, he found reason to ally with the Pilgrims against the hostile Naragansett tribe to the West. Massasoit's reputation as great friend of Plymouth Colony owed to his legendary courage, rectitude, and receptivity to colonial peace vows.

In the spirit of the coming together, Pilgrim leader Myles Standish (the *Mayflower*'s Stranger captain) and Massasoit made a peace and friendship agreement through which the Indians turned over the former Patuxet village land to the Pilgrims for their new Plymouth Plantation. Completed in March 1621, the accord pledged the two parties to not harm one another and to be allies in times of war.

Several months later Massasoit dispatched a second aide to Plymouth Plantation. His name was Hobomok. Hobomok advised the colony in establishing fur-trading posts throughout the Northeast. Thanks to profits from fur, Plymouth was able to meet its rising expenditures. Native know-how and willingness to share it were indispensable to the Pilgrims' survival.

By the fall of 1621, the Pilgrims had cause for good cheer. Their corn had grown high, their food supply would last the winter, and their good health they blessed in both church and wigwam. To rejoice in their bounty, they decided to hold a "thanks-giving" celebration. Governor Bradford chose December 13 as the date.

Just as the Puritans had long practiced thanksgiving rituals in England, the Algonquin nation, too, observed thanksgiving feasts.

On behalf of the Pilgrims, Captain Standish invited

Squanto, Massasoit, Samoset, and their families to attend the feast. The hosts were in for a surprise when ninety Wampanoag relatives showed up. Massasoit quickly set his men to work, and they returned with provisions that lasted well beyond the three days of feasting: deer, fish, beans, squash, corn soup, pumpkin, corn bread, berries, wild turkeys, ducks, geese, and swans.

Relations with the settlers were not without advantage to the natives. That the Pilgrims generally paid the former landowners for their new tracts may also have contributed to their initial welcome. But this begs the question, Did the natives and the Pilgrims agree on what *land purchase* meant? For the colonists, buying land bestowed ownership; for the Natives, however, it granted perpetual use of the terrain and resources. Ultimately, this discord would haunt settler-Indian relations for centuries to come.

As new waves of English settlers arrived, they pressed their advantages over the Native population, whose early assistance was soon forgotten. Just as the Puritans had been persecuted in Europe, they began disparaging and undermining Native religion and customs. Conversion of the indigenous "savages" to Christianity, a prime rationale for English colonization, predisposed the militant Puritans to disregard indigenous life.

After 1640, missionaries settled converts in small communities of "Praying Indians"—where the merest trace of their traditional ritual and faith resulted in expulsion, where Puritan attire and church attendance were mandatory, and where tribal culture and leadership were all but doomed to extinction.

Within a generation of the first Thanksgiving, whatever friendly feelings had existed between the Pilgrims and the natives gave way to sharp tensions. The balance of power had begun its inexorable shift in the settlers' favor.

By 1642, as many as twenty thousand freedom seekers had fled King Charles I's repressive England. Most were Anglican Puritans who were brought over by the joint stock venture known first as the Plymouth Colony and later as the Massachusetts Bay Company.

Conflicts also arose within the settler population. Bradford lamented the passing of the old "comfortable fellowship" as the church split into factions and Plymouthers departed for other parts of the continent seeking their "manifest destiny" of more land. On the Indian side, Massasoit's death in 1660 marked the last of the Wampanoags who felt loyally bound to the Pilgrims. Only three years earlier, Governor Bradford had also died.

Plymouth's city limits would bear Indian heads impaled on stakes as a totem of bicultural hostility. By

1675, New England witnessed the genocidal ravages known as King Philip's War. King Philip was also known as Metacomet, son of Massasoit. Unlike his father, Philip presided over a radicalization of Native policies and pledged to contain European expansion.

As the fur and wampum economy gave way to fishing and diversified trade, the Europeans no longer depended on wilderness skills to survive. Yet without the Natives' early generosity in sharing these skills, the forefathers may never have stood a chance on American shores.

~

Looking back on the history of Thanksgiving, several landmarks stand out. For example, the Massachusetts Bay Colony had known adversity from the outset, after their stormy voyage across the Atlantic. In gratitude of their safe landing, they set aside July 8, 1630, as a "daye of thanksgivinge in all the plantations."

Another memorable Thanksgiving fell in revolutionary times. Amid the bitter cold of 1777, General George Washington and his troops heeded the Continental Congress's decree to observe the first Thanksgiving of the newly established United States of America. They broke stride en route to Valley Forge, honor bound to celebrate.

President Washington designated November 26,

1789, a national day of "thanksgiving and prayer" and issued the first federal Thanksgiving Proclamation toasting our common national history around the ancestral harvest table. Our new form of government was what motivated his religious gratitude. Yet official thanks to God wasn't for everyone. In the early 1800s, President Jefferson scorned the notion, strictly upholding separation of church and state.

It wasn't until the latter half of the nineteenth century that our nation's leaders trained their nostalgia on the "first" American Thanksgiving. The spirit of that shared, multicultural feast in 1621 provided an ideal symbol of America's new self-image as a melting pot.

It was President Abraham Lincoln who anchored the tradition with his 1863 Thanksgiving Proclamation. His beliefs in maintaining national union during the War Between the States were clearly enunciated as he invited his "fellow citizens in every part of the United States . . . to set apart and observe the last Thursday of November next, as a day of Thanksgiving and Praise to our beneficent Father who dwelleth in the Heavens."

Roughly a decade after Lincoln's proclamation, another important Thanksgiving tradition was born with the November 1869 kickoff of the first intercollegiate football game; Rutgers University beat Princeton 6–4. Within several years, the game would take place on Thanksgiving Day.

Football was quickly anointed a national sport, causing a cranky *New York Herald* writer to lament some two decades later, "Thanksgiving Day is no longer a solemn festival to God for mercies given. . . . It is a holiday granted by the State and the Nation to see a game of football." By the time radio and television came along in the twentieth century, holiday audiences from coast to coast made good this inalienable right.

The first Thanksgiving Day parade filled the streets of Philadelphia in 1923. A roaring success, it inspired the Macy's Thanksgiving Day Parade the next year, and the next and the next to this very day.

Yet another piece of the Thanksgiving ritual fell into place with President Franklin D. Roosevelt in 1939. As a concession to retailers eager for a longer pre-Christmas selling season, FDR set Thanksgiving Day as the third Thursday in November. Though the popular hue and cry convinced Congress to reprise Lincoln's choice—the fourth Thursday—and commit it to law, ever since, Americans have patriotically shopped for Yuletide with a Thanksgiving glow.

Not every president has issued a Thanksgiving Proclamation, but especially poignant are those documenting our nation's history of war and peace.

Woodrow Wilson's proclamation of 1917 appeals to our custom of giving thanks "even in the midst of the tragedy of a world shaken by war and immeasurable disaster, in the midst of sorrow and great peril, because even amidst the darkness that has gathered about us we can see the great blessings God has bestowed upon us."

President Dwight D. Eisenhower sealed his 1953 proclamation with the invocation: "Especially we are grateful this year for the truce in battle-weary Korea, which gives anxious men and women throughout the world the hope that there may now be an enduring peace."

In the autumn following the 1991 Persian Gulf War, President George Bush expressed thanks that "we were spared the terrible consequences of a long and protracted struggle." A decade later, his son George W. Bush stated, "As we recover from the terrible tragedies of September 11, Americans of every belief and heritage give thanks to God for the many blessings we enjoy as a free, faithful and fair-minded land."

Quite a tradition. Yet, it's noteworthy that the so-called First Thanksgiving did not lead to an annual feast. Nor for that matter did the Pilgrims refer to it as a Thanksgiving Feast. On the contrary, for this pious sect, thanksgiving observances meant prayer and fasting; this was, after all, a sect that banned Christmas celebrations as debauchery. Nonetheless the 1621 festivities would be taken as the prototype of Thanksgiving Day in this country.

Evermore today, Americans happily recall the

Pilgrims' first Thanksgiving as emblematic of our national devotion.

From its checkered history of amity between the Europeans and Indians and subsequent stresses and strains, Thanksgiving has evolved into an event of great symbolism. We have transcended the past by bringing together family and friends for a ceremonial celebration, one where we always remember our reasons to be grateful, our home, and our bonds.

MAYFLOWER PASSENGER LIST

Fully one fourth of all Americans claim to be descendants of the *Mayflower* passengers. Are you one?

Four American presidents can trace their lineage back: Theodore Roosevelt and his cousin Franklin Delano Roosevelt as well as President George Bush Jr. and his son, George W. Their common *Mayflower* forebear was John Howland. And just think, Howland nearly drowned at sea during the crossing!

Nine American presidents can also trace ancestry to the Plymouth Colony Pilgrims. These include John Adams and his son John Quincy Adams, Zachary Taylor, Ulysses S. Grant, and James Garfield.

Here is a list of the 102 passengers who braved the rough Atlantic waters in pursuit of a new life. See if you recognize any of their names from your family tree.

John Alden
Isaac Allerton
Mary Allerton (wife)
Bartholomew Allerton (son)
Mary Allerton (daughter)
Remember Allerton (daughter)
John Allerton (no relation)
John Billington
Eleanor Billington (wife)
Francis Billington (son)
John Billington (son)
William Bradford
Dorothy Bradford (wife—died at sea))
William Brewster
Mary Brewster (wife)
Love Brewster (son)
Wrestling Brewster (son)
Richard Britteridge
Peter Browne
William Butten
Robert Carter
John Carver
Katherine Carver (wife)
James Chilton
Susanna Chilton (wife)
Mary Chilton (unknown relation)
Richard Clarke

Francis Cooke

John Cooke (son)

Humility Cooper

John Crackstone

Edward Doty

Francis Eaton

Sarah Eaton (first wife)

Dorothy Eaton (second wife)

Samuel Eaton (son)

(first name unknown) Ely (sailor)

Thomas English

Moses Fletcher

Edward Fuller

Ann Fuller (wife)

Samuel Fuller (son)

Samuel Fuller (not related—physician)

Richard Gardiner

John Goodman

William Holbeck

John Hooke

Stephen Hopkins

Elizabeth Hopkins (wife)

Giles Hopkins (son)

Constance Hopkins (daughter)

Damaris Hopkins (daughter)

Oceanis Hopkins (son—born during voyage)

John Howland

John Langmore

William Latham

Edward Leister

Edmund Margesson

Christopher Martin

Mary Martin (wife)

Desire Minter

Elinor More

Jasper More

Richard More

Mary More

William Mullins

Alice Mullins (wife)

Joseph Mullins (son)

Priscilla Mullins (daughter)

Degory Priest

Solomon Prower

John Rigsdale

Alice Rigsdale (wife)

Thomas Rogers

Joseph Rogers (son)

Henry Sampson

George Soule

Miles Standish

Rose Standish (wife)

Elias Story

Edward Thompson

Edward Tilley

Agnes Tilley (wife)
John Tilley
Joan Tilley (wife)
Elizabeth Tilley (daughter)
Thomas Tinker
(wife of Thomas Tinker)
(son of Thomas Tinker)
William Trevore
John Turner
(son of John Turner)
(son of John Turner)
Master Richard Warren
William White
Susanna White (wife)
Peregrine White (son)
Resolved White (son)
Roger Wilder
Thomas Williams
Edward Winslow
Elizabeth Winslow (wife)
Gilbert Winslow (brother)

THANKSGIVING AROUND THE WORLD

Harvest and celebration have always gone together, ever since pagan times.

In ancient Athens the Greeks honored Demeter, the

goddess of grain, at the festival of Thesmosphoria. The Romans held an annual thanksgiving banquet to their harvest deity, Ceres; and the Israelites built huts with the earth's bounty during Sukkoth, or the Feast of Tabernacles. Egypt under the Pharaoh reveled in music, dance, and sports honoring Min, the god of vegetation and fertility.

Different cultures around the world continue to observe formal thanksgiving. Today the Dutch celebrate the hay harvest; the Germans, Oktoberfest; the French, the Wheat Harvest; and the Pueblo Indians, the Green Corn Dance. In Japan during the Aoi Festival, Kyoto's shrines ritualize past years of relief from floods and storms. And in China, Harvest Moon revelers make merry with bright lanterns and moon cakes.

Each November, Americans join this vast and venerable tradition of harvest rites. Before the Pilgrims left England for America, they surely observed the Saxon Harvest Home festival, with its corn sheaves, fruit baskets, and church bells. And once here, they were probably aware of the celebration of the Iroquois nation, with its Great Feather Dance at the corn harvest. Their ceremony for the Great Spirit included a prayer of thanks for the warmth of the sun, the light of the moon, water, game, herbs, flowers, maple sugar—and for the simple fact of being alive.

But by no means is harvest bounty the only occasion for thanksgiving. People around the world gather to offer thanks for personal, spiritual, and political blessings at various times of the year, often in hopes of overcoming bad fortune—or of extending good fortune.

Eight countries observe an official Thanksgiving Day: Argentina, Brazil, Canada, Japan, Korea, Liberia, Switzerland and, of course, the U.S.A.

The Thanksgiving
Ceremony

THE FORMAL CEREMONY THAT FOLLOWS IS designed to be read aloud by all around the Thanksgiving table. One person, the "leader," serves as master of ceremonies and directs the narrative when necessary. The Ceremony is designed to include everyone at the table—young and old alike. Participants take turns reading short passages, sometimes in unison, and perform activities, such as toasts and passing the harvest bowl. And, of course, the Ceremony includes the joy of song. On key or off-key, all share in.

Why add "Ceremony"—either formal or informal—to the Thanksgiving meal?

Many meals with family and friends are preceded by a simple grace, prayer, or toast. Thanksgiving is unique and special. It is the only holiday centered on a meal that also incorporates all Americans of all religions and ethnic backgrounds.

Christmas and Easter have meals, but they are incidental to Christian Church worship. Memorial Day, Independence Day, Labor Day, President's Day,

and Martin Luther King's birthday are mostly celebrated outside the home.

New Year's Eve is communal, but less unifying
of young and old (because of the hour), although it
is hard to resist a tear when all join in for "Auld
Lang Syne."

The Passover seder combines the elements of ceremony, history, appreciation, song, religious commitment, and a bountiful meal. This Thanksgiving
Ceremony translates that spirit for all Americans.

Besides, in a long life of attending, and hosting,
dinner parties, my wife and I remember the most
successful as those where the entire table participated
in a conversation about a meaningful subject (with a
toast, of course, to the host or hostess).

For our readers, the Thanksgiving meal is served
immediately after the following Ceremony, which
should take about twenty minutes.

~

*Preparations for the feast are complete; friends/family,
gathered; greetings, exchanged. The Thanksgiving table
is decked out for the occasion.*

*Ceremonial touches include one unlit candle, a large
bowl of fresh and dried fruit, bowls of nuts and
grapes. Also set, in the center, is a plate, empty except
for either five kernels of corn, five grains of rice, or*

five dried beans. This plate is symbolic of the Pilgrims' year of famine in the New World before the bountiful harvest celebrated at their first American Thanksgiving in 1621. It also reminds us that hunger persists today.

LEADER

Welcome, everyone, to our _____ (first, second, third, etc.) annual Thanksgiving Celebration. Today we are joined in common gratitude and affection for our good fortune in America. We celebrate another year of well-being, with hopes for the next year. Thank you all for joining my *(wife/husband/friend/mother/father/partner/_____)* and me on this special occasion.

We are all committed to democracy and freedom.

Though we celebrate with all those present, we also acknowledge those who could not be here today, and we remember those who are no longer with us. Please join me in a moment of silent recollection of the people we love and admire who aren't with us today.

After a moment of silence, the Leader resumes.

Let's toast our new tradition of Thanksgiving for bringing together close family and friends.

And let's toast our great country. Cheers to Thanksgiving Day!

[All toast]

LEADER

We will now recount the history of this great holiday by reading as we proceed around the table, starting with *(insert name)* on my right. Please begin:

FIRST READER, to the right of the Leader

We gather on this day of Thanksgiving to recall the early history of our nation. We express heartfelt thanks for our many blessings—past, present, and future—in the company of our friends and family.

NEXT READER, to the right of the First Reader

As the Pilgrims of Plymouth Colony celebrated their first Thanksgiving, in 1621, they had many reasons to be grateful. They had come to this continent to flee religious persecution in their home country of England.

NEXT READER

In the course of their perilous journey to freedom, the staunch believers had endured

eleven years of exile in Holland . . . sixty-six days
at sea aboard the *Mayflower* . . . and a year of
famine on American soil. The cost of their
religious freedom was high: Fewer than half the
original *Mayflower* settlers survived their first
winter in the New World.

NEXT READER
_____

But those who survived were grateful for their
good fortune. They had forged a close
friendship with the local Wampanoag tribe,
whose custom was to help visitors. Many
indigenous people had already perished from
diseases brought to the New World by earlier
European visitors.

NEXT READER
_____

Those Natives who survived helped the Pilgrims
adjust to their new home, teaching them how to
cultivate corn, to net fish, and to build shelters to
protect them from the harsh weather. Much of
the Pilgrims' settlement had been developed by
Native Americans.

NEXT READER
_____

Thanks to the warmth and generosity of their
Native hosts, the Pilgrims were able to plant and
reap their first crop in the New World. In return,

they invited the Native Americans to share in
their harvest festival.

NEXT READER

Sharing in blessings is at the heart of
Thanksgiving and the American spirit. At
Thanksgiving this year, and every year, we
carry on the American tradition of giving and
sharing.

NEXT READER

We gather to reinforce the ties of family,
friendship, and community. With this celebration,
we all reach out in gratitude to our fellow
Americans beyond this table, and acknowledge
that, together, we make up the great national
family.

NEXT READER, pointing to the plate

The near-empty plate at the center of this table
represents the year of famine suffered by the
Pilgrims when they first arrived in Plymouth.
There was not enough food, but there were seeds
for the future. Had it not been for the Native
people, the Pilgrims might have perished in
starvation. Today we honor the sacred bond of
friendship among the first Americans and among
ourselves today.

The Thanksgiving Ceremony

NEXT READER

Let us praise the settlers of New England and the 59
Natives who helped them. They symbolize all
brave immigrants from the world over, who risked
adversity to come and settle in America. We <u>all</u>
came in the pursuit of freedom, opportunity, and
happiness.

NEXT READER

We now ask *(insert name of oldest participant)* to
light the ceremonial candle. *(Same name)* is the
oldest person present, and *(his/her)* life experience
provides us with a guiding light. The youngest
person, *(insert name)*, will blow out the candle
after the meal.

[The oldest person at the table lights the ceremonial candle.]

NEXT READER, as the oldest lights the candle

We ask you, *(name of oldest person at the table)*, to
recall the words of William Bradford, in honor of
the candle lighting. Bradford was governor of
Plymouth Colony and recorded those early
American years in his journal *Of Plymouth Plantation*.

OLDEST PERSON

"Thus out of small beginnings, greater things
have been produced by His hand, that made all

things that are . . . and as one small candle may light a thousand, so the light here kindled hath shone unto many . . . yea, in some sort, to our whole nation."

LEADER

We will now continue the reading, moving around the table counterclockwise, beginning with *(insert name)*.

NEXT READER

As the years passed, the Pilgrims settled in to their new home. But their strict customs no longer accommodated others whose beliefs were different. What began in a spirit of sharing and friendship between the Pilgrims and the Natives, ended in conflict.

NEXT READER

Nevertheless, the Pilgrims remain a symbol of the many different people who have come here seeking opportunity, freedom of expression and religion, and the pursuit of happiness that our constitution has since granted to us.

NEXT READER

On this Thursday, the _____ day of November, in the year two thousand and _____, we gather

to pay tribute to those of all beliefs who have
come here.

NEXT READER

We gratefully acknowledge the efforts and
sacrifices of our leaders, and of ordinary people,
who created and maintained the spirit of peace
and friendship on which this great nation was
founded.

NEXT READER

In her poem *The New Colossus: The Statue of Liberty*,
Emma Lazarus wrote:
"Not like the brazen giant of Greek fame,
With conquering limbs astride from land to land;
Here at our sea-washed, sunset gates shall stand
A mighty woman with a torch, whose flame
Is the imprisoned lightning, and her name
Mother of Exiles. From her beacon-hand
Glows worldwide welcome;
    her mild eyes command
The air-bridged harbor that twin cities frame.

NEXT READER

"'Keep ancient lands, your storied pomp!' cries she
With silent lips. 'Give me your tired, your poor,
Your huddled masses yearning to breathe free,
The wretched refuse of your teeming shore.

The Thanksgiving Ceremony

Send these, the homeless, tempest-tossed to me.
I lift my lamp beside the golden door.'"

62

NEXT READER

These words are inscribed on the Statue of Liberty. It stands in New York Harbor as a shining symbol of the many different paths to Thanksgiving in America. Over the years, our nation has taken in newcomers from all over the world. Some were welcomed; many were not; others came under force. Very few actually descended from the *Mayflower*.

NEXT READER

Many were brought in chains to serve as slaves, and not as free citizens.

NEXT READER

Many fled ethnic persecution, political oppression, famine, or annihilation.

NEXT READER

Still others came in pursuit of economic opportunity. Many came simply because adventure beckoned. And many, of course, were born here. <u>All of us</u> have ancestors from other lands.

NEXT READER

As we celebrate Thanksgiving, let us remember
that while Americans are an independent people,
we are also interdependent. Our greatest
achievements are those we have accomplished
together, pooling our skills, our traditions, our
knowledge.

NEXT READER

Harvest festivals are celebrated in all cultures.
Ours is intended to add special recognition of
America's blessings.

LEADER

We now pass the harvest bowl. As each of us
takes something from it, we share in the bounty
of the harvest.

*[A bowl filled with nuts and fresh and dried fruits is
passed around the table. After everyone has taken from it,
the celebration continues.]*

[Optional]

LEADER

We now invite each child or young person to ask
one question about Thanksgiving or American

history. Any other participant is welcome to provide the answer. Let's begin with *(a designated child/young person)*.

[The leader facilitates the questions and answers. At the conclusion, the leader resumes.]

LEADER

We will resume the reading of the ceremony with *(name of reader to the right of the last reader)*.

NEXT READER

Ever since the first Thanksgiving, Americans have offered thanks to God and to one another for their well-being. But it was our first president, George Washington, who proclaimed the fourth Thursday of November as a national day of Thanksgiving. Most presidents, since Washington, have issued proclamations of thanks for the blessings particular to that year.

Here are brief excerpts from Lincoln's famous Thanksgiving Proclamation, issued in hopes of national unity, during the War Between the States. The date was October 3, 1863.

NEXT READER

"The year that is drawing to its close, has been filled with the blessings of fruitful fields and healthful skies. To these bounties . . . which are so constantly enjoyed that we are prone to forget the source from which they come . . . others have been added . . . of so extraordinary a nature, that they cannot fail to penetrate, and soften, even the heart which is habitually insensible . . . to the ever watchful providence of Almighty God . . .

NEXT READER

"The gracious gifts of the Most High God . . . should be solemnly, reverently and gratefully acknowledged . . . as with one heart and one voice by the whole American People.

NEXT READER

"Heal the wounds of the nation . . . and restore it . . . to the full enjoyment of peace, harmony, tranquility and Union."

NEXT READER

We give thanks for the collective blessings we share. But this holiday is also about the unique blessings and talents we each bring to the table, as individuals.

LEADER

We now go around the table, each one of us sharing one blessing for which we are personally

grateful today. Let's start with *(insert name)*, who
sits to my right.

EACH PARTICIPANT

I give thanks for . . .

LEADER

We all give thanks for the diversity of the
American people as eloquently expressed by
Martin Luther King Jr.

NEXT READER

"I have a dream that one day this nation will rise
up and live out the true meaning of its creed:
'We hold these truths to be self-evident: that all
men are created equal.' . . . This is our hope . . .
With this faith we will be able to hew out of the
mountain of despair a stone of hope. With this
faith we will be able to transform the jangling
discords of our nation into a beautiful symphony
of brotherhood."

NEXT READER

The diversity of our people is one of our greatest
resources. But there are also many others to
which we pay tribute. All have attracted such
varied peoples to our shores.

The Thanksgiving Ceremony

FIRST READER

We give thanks for and pledge the purity of
our water;

NEXT READER

the richness of our soil;

NEXT READER

the navigability of our lakes and rivers;

NEXT READER

the coastline bordering great and protective seas;

NEXT READER

the abundance of our minerals;

NEXT READER

the depth of our forests;

NEXT READER

the skill of our country's farmers and laborers;

NEXT READER

the energy of our builders;

NEXT READER

the enterprise of our business people;

NEXT READER

the joy produced by our artists;

NEXT READER

the wisdom of our teachers, clergy, scientists,
and leaders.

NEXT READER

Preserving the vast beauty and scope of our
country's landscapes and working to improve the
livability of our cities—home to the diverse peoples
who have come, settled, and flourished here.

NEXT READER

Let us all toast the sweet goodness of these
resources and great accomplishments of our
people—by symbolically savoring the grapes from
the vine.

[All take grapes from the bowl.]

NEXT READER

We have given thanks for the perseverance of the
early settlers, the diversity of our people and the
richness of our land. Let us also remember that
our many blessings have also created a nation
with unique responsibilities and leadership
throughout the world.

NEXT READER

We give thanks that, in simpler times, our
oceans kept us safe, so that only our own
war was fought on our own land. Today,
those oceans no longer provide total safety.
We commit ourselves to unite with other
peace lovers throughout the world for mutual
security.

NEXT READER

Let us now give thanks for our political,
economic, and social democracy. It undergirds
and enhances all our opportunities in business,
the arts, sciences, technology, and education.
Let us read together Thomas Jefferson's words
from The Declaration of Independence:

ALL READ IN UNISON.

"We hold these truths to be self-evident, that all
men are created equal. That they are endowed
by their Creator with certain unalienable Rights.
That among these are Life, Liberty, and the
pursuit of Happiness."

LEADER

May we live our lives throughout the year in the
same spirit of thanks and goodwill that we have
experienced here today. Now, let us join hands

for the reading of the Thanksgiving grace,
by Robert Louis Stevenson.

ALL READ IN UNISON

"Behold our family [and friends] here assembled.
We thank Thee for this place in which we dwell;
for the love that unites us, for the peace accorded
us this day; for the hope with which we expect
the morrow, for the health, the work, the food
and the bright skies that make our lives
delightful; and for our friends in all parts of the
earth. Let peace abound in our small company."

LEADER

We now celebrate in song—the first verse and
chorus of "America the Beautiful."

ALL SING IN UNISON

O beautiful for spacious skies,
For amber waves of grain,
For purple mountain majesties
Above the fruited plain!

America! America!
God shed His grace on Thee,
And crown thy good with brotherhood
From sea to shining sea!

LEADER

The Thanksgiving Ceremony is now concluded. Let us all now share the bounty of our Thanksgiving dinner.

[DINNER IS THEN SERVED.]

[Optional]

LEADER

Our Thanksgiving Celebration is now concluded. With our appetites satisfied, let's go around the table and each make a pledge for the upcoming year. I will begin, and then *(insert name)* will continue, as the person to my right, and so on. Each promise should reflect a goal you hope to achieve in the coming year. We will conclude with the youngest, *(insert name)*, who will blow out the ceremonial candle after all promises are made.

EACH PARTICIPANT

I promise to . . .

[Going around the table, each participant makes a promise. Youngest blows out the candle.]

The Thanksgiving Ceremony

LEADER

Thank you.

[Participants decide whether to continue with songs, hymns, prayers, readings, poetry, games, or . . . football. Additional material follows in the next chapter.]

Inspirational
Thanksgiving
Material

WE'VE DEVELOPED THE THANKSGIVING ceremony for American celebrants from many diverse cultures. To tailor it to your tastes, or simply to add spice from year to year, draw from the following cornucopia: observances, short thoughts, prayers, poems, songs and hymns, proclamations, or the preceding historic passages. Each selection has been chosen to reflect Thanksgiving themes of gratitude, joy, seasonal pleasures, and American values.

Of course, these refrains can be mixed as their own ceremony or added to the formal Ceremony, before or after dinner.

SHORT THOUGHTS

For your Thanksgiving greetings and toasts, or if you're creating your own Ceremony, here are some appropriate thoughts:

Gratitude is the sign of noble souls.

Aesop, "Androcles," *Fables*

Grateful Praise alone due to God, the Lord and Nourisher of the worlds.

Koran

Let us be grateful to people who make us happy; they are the charming gardeners who make our souls blossom.

Marcel Proust

God is pleased with no music below so much as with the thanksgiving songs of relieved widows and supported orphans; of rejoicing, comforted and thankful persons.

Jeremy Taylor, seventeenth-century
Unitarian Universalist minister

I will praise God's name in song and glorify him with thanksgiving.

Psalm 69:30

A noble person is thankful and mindful of the favors he receives from others.

The Buddha

Gratitude is a quality similar to electricity: it must be produced and discharged and used up in order to exist at all.

William Faulkner

To educate yourself for the feeling of gratitude means to take nothing for granted, but to always seek out and value the kind that will stand behind the action. Nothing that is done for you is a matter of course. Everything originates in a will for the good, which is directed at you. Train yourself never to put off the word or action for the expression of gratitude.

> Albert Schweitzer, humanitarian, theologian,
> and medical doctor

I do not think of all the misery, but of the glory that remains. Go outside into the fields, nature and the sun, go out and seek happiness in yourself and in God. Think of the beauty that again and again discharges itself within and without you and be happy.

> Anne Frank, *The Diary of Anne Frank*

Let us remember that, as much has been given us, much will be expected from us, and that true homage comes from the heart as well as from the lips, and shows itself in deeds.

> Theodore Roosevelt, Thanksgiving Proclamation, 1901

If the only prayer you say in your whole life is "thank you," that would suffice.

> Meister Eckehart, Christian mystic

The Thanksgiving Ceremony

As we express our gratitude, we must never forget that the highest appreciation is not to utter words, but to live by them.

> John F. Kennedy

This is what binds all people and all creation together—the gratuity of the gift of being.

> Matthew Fox, spiritual theologian,
> The Humble Approach Initiative

There are two ways to live your life. One is as though nothing is a miracle. The other is as though everything is a miracle.

> Albert Einstein

As I express my gratitude, I become more deeply aware of it. And the greater my awareness, the greater my need to express it. What happens here is a spiraling ascent, a process of growth in ever expanding circles around a steady center.

> Brother David Steindl-Rast,
> *Gratefulness: The Heart of Prayer*

Gratitude is more than a word or gesture. . . . Gratitude is a state of consciousness. It is an experience of living in a state of joy.

> Iyanla Vanzant, Yoruba priestess and author

A heart filled with gratitude and thanksgiving fills
the whole being with song—an anticipation of life's
happiness and peace.

Declaration of World Thanksgiving, 1995

. . . Not yesterday I learned to know
The love of bare November days
Before the coming of the snow . . .

Robert Frost, *My November Guest*

Our Creator shall continue to dwell above the sky,
and that is where those on earth will end their
thanksgiving.

Seneca Nation of the Iroquois Confederacy

O Lord, that lends me life, lend me a heart replete
with thankfulness.

William Shakespeare, *King Henry VI*

A thankful heart is not only the greatest of virtues,
but the parent of all the others.

Cicero

No matter what our situation, whether we are rich
or poor, educated or not, of one race, gender,
religion or another, we all desire to be happy and to
avoid suffering.

Dalai Lama

The Thanksgiving Ceremony

How wonderful it would be if we could help our children and grandchildren to learn thanksgiving at an early age. Thanksgiving opens the doors. It changes a child's personality. A child is resentful, negative—or thankful. Thankful children want to give, they radiate happiness, they draw people.

Sir John Marks Templeton, philanthropist,
Is Progress Speeding Up?: Our Multitudes of Blessings

[Appreciation] makes immortal all that is best and most beautiful. . . . It exalts the beauty of that which is beautiful. . . . It strips the veil of familiarity from the world, and lays bare and naked sleeping beauty, which is in the spirit of its forms.

Percy Bysshe Shelley, *Ode to the West Wind*

Joy is prayer—Joy is strength—Joy is love—Joy is a net of love by which you can catch souls. She gives most who gives with joy.

Mother Teresa

We must become the change we want to see.

Mahatma Gandhi

One can never pay in gratitude; one can only pay "in kind" somewhere else in life.

Anne Morrow Lindberg

What I kept, I lost.
What I spent, I had.
What I gave, I have.

Persian Proverb

God loves a cheerful giver. She gives most who gives
with joy. The best way to show our gratitude to God
and the people is to accept everything with joy.

Mother Teresa, *"Joy," A Gift for God*

A man who possesses genius is insufferable unless
he also possesses at least two other things: gratitude
and cleanliness.

Friedrich Nietzsche

A man's indebtedness is not virtue; his repayment
is. Virtue begins when he dedicates himself actively
to the job of gratitude.

Ruth Benedict, *The Chrysanthemum and the Sword*

It is most appropriate that a people whose
storehouses have been so lavishly filled with all the
fruits of the earth by the gracious favor of God
should manifest their gratitude by large gifts to His
suffering children in other lands.

Benjamin Harrison, U.S. president, Special Message to
Congress during famine in Russia

The Thanksgiving Ceremony

A grateful mind
By owing owes not, but still pays, at once
Indebted and discharg'd.

John Milton, *Paradise Lost*

To give thanks in solitude is enough. Thanksgiving
has wings and goes where it must go. Your prayer
knows much more about it than you do.

Victor Hugo, *L'Homme qui rit*

Gratitude to gratitude always gives birth.

Sophocles

Let us first resolve: First to attain the grace of
silence; Second to deem all fault-finding that does
no good a sin. . . . Third to practice the grace and
virtue of praise.

Harriet Beecher Stowe

PRAYERS AND REFLECTIONS

While the storm clouds gather
Far across the sea,
Let us swear allegiance
To a land that's free;
Let us all be grateful
For a land so fair,
As we raise our voices
In a solemn prayer.

Irving Berlin, spoken introduction to "God Bless America"

The Pilgrim: a simple people, inspired by an ardent
faith in God, a dauntless courage in danger, a
boundless resourcefulness in the face of difficulties,
an impregnable fortitude in adversity: thus they
have in some measure become the spiritual ancestors
of all Americans.

Samuel Eliot Morison,
1954 introduction to *Of Plymouth Plantation*

Celebrate . . . after you have gathered the produce
of your threshing floor and your winepress.
Be joyful at your Feast—you, your sons and
daughters . . . God will bless you in all your harvest
and in all the work of your hands, and your joy will
be complete.

Deuteronomy 16:13–17, Jewish Sukkoth

The Thanksgiving Ceremony

The LORD is my shepherd; I shall not want.

He maketh me to lie down in green pastures: he
    leadeth me beside the still waters.

He restoreth my soul: he leadeth me in the paths
    of righteousness for his name's sake.

Yea, though I walk through the valley of the
    shadow of death, I will fear no evil: for thou art
    with me; thy rod and thy staff they comfort me.

Thou preparest a table before me in the presence
    of mine enemies: thou anointest my head with
    oil; my cup runneth over.

Surely goodness and mercy shall follow me all the
    days of my life: and I will dwell in the house of
    the LORD for ever.

Psalm 23, Book of Common Prayer

May the road rise to meet you,
May the wind be always at your back,
May the sun shine warm on your face,
The rain fall softly on your fields;
And until we meet again,
May God hold you in the palm of His hand.
Amen.

An Irish blessing

Behold our family here assembled.
We thank thee for this place in which we dwell;   85
for the love that unites us;
for the peace accorded us this day;
for the hope with which we expect the morrow;
for the health, the work, the food, and the
     bright skies
that make our lives delightful;
for our friends in all parts of the earth;
and for our friendly helpers in this foreign isle.

   Robert Louis Stevenson, *Treasure Island*

Our Father, who art in heaven,
Hallowed be thy Name.
Thy kingdom come.
Thy will be done,
On earth as it is in heaven.
Give us this day our daily bread.
And forgive us our trespasses,
As we forgive those who trespass against us.
And lead us not into temptation,
But deliver us from evil.
For thine is the kingdom, and the power,
     and the glory, for ever and ever.
Amen.

   The Lord's Prayer, Book of Common Prayer

Almighty God, who hast given us this good land
   for our heritage;

We humbly beseech thee that we may always
   prove ourselves a people mindful of thy favor
   and glad to do thy will.

Bless our land with honorable industry, sound
   learning and pure manners.

Save us from violence, discord and confusion;
   from pride and arrogancy and from every
   evil way.

Defend our liberties, and fashion into one united
   people the multitudes brought hither out of
   many kindreds and tongues.

Endure with the spirit of wisdom those to whom
   in thy Name we entrust the authority of
   government, that there may be justice and
   peace at home, and that through obedience to
   thy law, we may show forth thy praise among
   the nations of the earth.

In the time of prosperity, fill our hearts with
   thankfulness, and in the day of trouble, suffer
   not our trust in thee to fail.

Amen.

   Prayer for Our Country, Book of Common Prayer

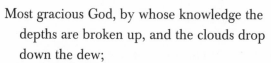

Most gracious God, by whose knowledge the
   depths are broken up, and the clouds drop
   down the dew;

We yield thee unfeigned thanks and praise for the
   seed-time and harvest, for the increase of the
   ground and the gathering in of the fruits
   thereof, and for all the other blessings of thy
   merciful providence bestowed upon this nation
   and people.

And, we beseech thee, give us just sense of these
   great mercies;

such as may appear in our lives by an humble,
   holy and obedient walking before thee all
   our days.

Amen.

> Prayer to Almighty God for the Fruits of the Earth
> and all the Other Blessings of His Merciful Providence,
> Book of Common Prayer

. . . You said that we should always be thankful
For our earth and for each other
So it is that we are gathered here
We are your children, Lord of the sky . . .
We speak to you through the rising smoke
We are thankful, Lord of the Sky.

> A Thanksgiving Prayer from the Iroquois (Seneca)
> people, excerpt translated by Chuck Larsen

The Thanksgiving Ceremony

That's the time to give and receive thanks,
a national holiday for America,
a symbol of America's culture,
an ideal to teach our children,
a happy time for family gatherings.

Thanksgiving is for giving thanks,
remembering the Pilgrims launching the day,
a tribute to the leaders of our nation,
gratitude for our freedom and our opportunities.

We give thanks for the privilege of saying it,
writing it, singing it, praying it
to all our friends and neighbors
who do so much for us.

Our lives overflow with good things,
the beauty of nature—rainbows and sunsets
     and roses,
we look in awe, admiring each one,
thanking God who gave them.

Prayer is the simple line between God and us.
let us use it till we get the habit
to say "Thank you, God" every day, every night,
all our life.

Samuel F. Pugh, *Thanksgiving Day*

O God, when I have food,
help me to remember the hungry;
When I have work,
help me to remember the jobless;
When I have a home,
help me to remember those who have
   no home at all;
When I am without pain,
help me to remember those who suffer.
And remembering,
help me to destroy my complacency;
bestir my compassion,
and be concerned enough to help;
By word and deed,
those who cry out for what we take for granted.
Amen.

   Samuel F. Pugh, *A Thanksgiving Prayer*

Lord, be with us on this day of Thanksgiving,
Help us make the most of this life we are living.
As we are about to partake of this bountiful meal
Let us not forget the needy and the hunger
   they feel.
Help us to show compassion in all that we do,
And for all our many blessings we say thank You.
   Amen.

   Helen Latham

The Thanksgiving Ceremony

O Thou Kind Lord! This gathering is turning to
Thee. These hearts are radiant with Thy love.
These minds and spirits are exhilarated by the
message of Thy glad-tidings. O God! Let this
American democracy become glorious in spiritual
degrees even as it has aspired to material degrees,
and render this just government victorious. Confirm
this reverend nation to upraise the standard of the
oneness of humanity, to promulgate the Most Great
Peace, to become thereby most glorious and
praiseworthy among all the nations of the world.
O God! This American nation is worthy of Thy
favors and is deserving of Thy mercy. Make it
precious and near to Thee through Thy bounty and
bestowal.

Abdu'l-Bahá, O Thou Kind Lord!

Praised be Thou, O Lord our God, King of
    the universe, Who sanctified us with His
    commandments and commanded us to kindle
    festival lights.
Praised be Thou, O Lord our God, King of the
    universe, Who gave us life, and sustained us,
    and enabled us to reach this season of joy.
    Candlelighting Blessing translated from the Hebrew

We return thanks to our mother, the earth, which
sustains us.

We return thanks to the rivers and streams, which
supply us with water.

We return thanks to all herbs, which furnish
medicines for the cure of our diseases.

We return thanks to the moon and stars, which
have given to us their light when the sun
was gone.

We return thanks to the sun, that has looked upon
the earth with a beneficent eye.

Lastly, we return thanks to the Great Spirit, in
Whom is embodied all goodness, and Who
directs all things for the good of Her children.

Iroquois Prayer, adapted by the Sisters of St. Joseph
of Peace

When you reap the harvest of your land, you shall
not reap all the way to the edges of your field, or
gather the gleanings of your harvest. You shall not
pick your vineyard bare, or gather the fallen fruit of
your vineyard; you shall leave them for the poor
and the stranger.

Leviticus 19:9–10

The Thanksgiving Ceremony

Our Father and Our God,

. . . We praise You for Your goodness to our
    nation, giving us blessings far beyond
    what we deserve.

Yet we know all is not right with America.
We deeply need a moral and spiritual renewal
to help us meet the many problems we face.

Convict of us sin. Help us to turn to You in
repentance and faith. Set our feet on the
path of Your righteousness and peace.

We pray today for our nation's leaders.
Give them the wisdom to know what
is right, and the courage to do it.

You have said, "Blessed is the nation whose
God is the Lord." May this be a new era
for America, as we humble ourselves and
    acknowledge You alone as
our Savior and Lord. . . .

    Billy Graham, *Prayer for the Nation*

Blessed are you, Ruler of the Universe, for keeping
us in life, for sustaining us and for helping us reach
this moment.

She-he-hayanu Prayer, Jewish Sukkoth

We have come to this Rock, to record here our
homage for our Pilgrim Fathers; our sympathy in
their sufferings; our gratitude for their labors; our
admiration of their virtues; our veneration for their
piety; and our attachment to those principles of civil
and religious liberty, which they encountered the
dangers of the ocean, the storms of heaven, the
violence of savages, disease, exile, and famine, to
enjoy and establish. And we would leave here, also,
for the generations which are rising up rapidly to fill
our places, some proof, that we have endeavored to
transmit the great inheritance unimpaired; that in
our estimate of public principles, and private virtue;
in our veneration of religion and piety; in our
devotion to civil and religious liberty; in our regard
to whatever advances human knowledge, or
improves human happiness, we are not altogether
unworthy of our origin. . . .

Daniel Webster, nationalist, statesman,
lawyer, and orator

POEMS

"I Hear America Singing"
BY WALT WHITMAN

I hear America singing, the varied carols I hear;

Those of mechanics—each one singing his, as it
    should be, blithe and strong;

The carpenter singing his, as he measures his
    plank or beam,

The mason singing his, as he makes ready for
    work, or leaves off work,

The boatman singing what belongs to him in his
    boat—the deckhand singing on the steamboat
    deck;

The shoemaker singing as he sits on his bench—
    the hatter singing as he stands;

The wood-cutter's song—the ploughboy's, on his
    way in the morning, or at the noon
    intermission, or at sundown;

The delicious singing of the mother—or of the
    young wife at work—or of the girl sewing

Or washing—Each singing what belongs to her,
    and to none else;

The day what belongs to the day—At night, the
    party of young fellows, robust, friendly,

Singing, with open mouths, their strong
    melodious songs.

From "Contradictions: Tracking Poems," III, 28

BY ADRIENNE RICH

This high summer we love will pour its light
the fields grown rich and ragged in one strong
   moment
then before we're ready will crash into autumn
with a violence we can't accept
a bounty we can't forgive
Night frost will strike when the noons are warm
the pumpkins wildly glowing   the green
   tomatoes
straining huge on the vines
queen anne and blackeyed susan will straggle rusty
as the milkweed stakes her claim
she who will stand at last   dark sticks barely
   rising
up through the snow   her testament of
   continuation
We'll dream of a longer summer
But this is the one we have:
I lay my sunburnt hand
on your table: this is the time we have.

From "The Pumpkin"
BY JOHN GREENLEAF WHITTIER

Ah! on Thanksgiving Day, when from East and
    from West,
From North and from South, come the pilgrim
    and guest,
When the gray-haired New Englander sees round
    his board
The old broken links of affection restored,
When the care-wearied man seeks his mother
    once more,
And the worn matron smiles where the girl
    smiled before—
What moistens the lip and what brightens the eye?
What calls back the past, like the rich pumpkin pie?

From "We Have a Beautiful Mother"
BY ALICE WALKER

. . . We have a beautiful
mother
Her green lap
immense
Her brown embrace
eternal
Her blue body
everything
we know.

"Black Family Pledge"
BY MAYA ANGELOU

Because we have forgotten our ancestors our
children no longer give us honor.

Because we have lost the path our ancestors
cleared, kneeling in perilous undergrowth, our
children cannot find their way.

Because we have banished the God of our
ancestors, our children can not pray.

Because the long wails of our ancestors have
faded beyond our hearing, our children cannot
hear us crying.

Because we have abandoned our wisdom of
mothering and fathering, our befuddled
children give birth to children they neither
want nor understand.

Because we have forgotten how to love, the
adversary is within our gates, and holds us up
to the mirror of the world, shouting, Regard the
loveless.

Therefore, we pledge to bind ourselves again to
one another;

To embrace our lowliest,

To keep company with our loneliest,

To educate our illiterate,

To feed our starving,

(continued)

To clothe our ragged,

To do all good things, knowing that we are more
than keepers of our brothers and sisters. We are
our brothers and sisters.

In honor of those who toiled and implored God
with golden tongues, and in gratitude to the
same God who brought us out of hopeless
desolation,

We make this pledge.

"We Thank Thee"

BY RALPH WALDO EMERSON

For flowers that bloom about our feet;
For tender grass, so fresh, so sweet;
For song of bird, and hum of bee;
For all things fair we hear or see,
Father in heaven, we thank Thee!

For blue of stream and blue of sky;
For pleasant shade of branches high;
For fragrant air and cooling breeze;
For beauty of the blooming trees,
Father in heaven, we thank Thee!

From "Thanksgiving Day"
BY EMILY DICKINSON

One Day is there of the Series
Termed Thanksgiving Day.
Celebrated part at Table,
Part in Memory.

Neither Patriarch nor Pussy
I dissect the Play
Seems it to my Hooded thinking,
Reflex Holiday.

Had there been no sharp Subtraction
From the early Sum—
Not an Acre or a Caption
Where was once a Room—

Not a Mention, whose small Pebble
Wrinkled any Sea,
Unto Such, were such Assembly,
Twere Thanksgiving Day.

The Thanksgiving Ceremony

"Perhaps the World Ends Here"
BY JOY HARJO

The world begins at a kitchen table. No matter
what, we must eat to live.

The gifts of the earth are brought and prepared,
set on the table. So it has been since creation,
and it will go on.

We chase chickens or dogs away from it. Babies
teethe at the corners. They scrape their knees
under it.

It is here that children are given instruction on
what it means to be human. We make men at
it, we make women.

At this table we gossip, recall enemies and the
ghosts of lovers.

Our dreams drink coffee with us as they put their
arms around our children. They laugh with us
at our poor falling-down selves and as we put
ourselves back together once again at the table.

(continued)

This table has been a house in the rain, an
umbrella in the sun.

Wars have begun and ended at this table. It is a
place to hide in the shadow of terror. A place
to celebrate the terrible victory.

We have given birth on this table, and have
prepared our parents for burial here.

At this table we sing with joy, with sorrow. We
pray of suffering and remorse. We give thanks.

Perhaps the world will end at the kitchen table,
while we are laughing and crying, eating of the
last sweet bite.

From "Ode to the Americas"

BY PABLO NERUDA

... Americas,
in our orbit
the star of the people
is rising,
heroes are being born,
new paths being garlanded
with victory,
the ancient nations,
live again,
autumn passes
in the most radiant light,
new flags
flutter in the wind.
May your voice and your deeds,
America,
rise from your green girdle,
may there be an end
to love imprisoned,
may your native dignity
be restored,
may your grain rise toward the sky
awaiting with other nations
the inevitable dawn.

From "Earth"

BY KAHLIL GIBRAN

. . . How beautiful you are, Earth, and how sublime!

How perfect is your obedience to the light, and
How noble is your submission to the sun!

How lovely you are, veiled in shadow, and how
Charming your face, masked with obscurity!

How soothing is the song of your dawn, and how
harsh are the praises of your eventide!
How perfect you are, Earth, and how majestic!

I have seen the fruits of your summer labor.
In Autumn, in your vineyards, I saw your
blood flow as wine.
Your winter carried me into your bed, where the
   snow
Attested to your purity.
In your Spring you are an aromatic essence; in
   your
Summer you are generous; in your Autumn you
   are
A source of plenty . . .

(continued)

The Thanksgiving Ceremony

(continued)

. . . How generous you are, Earth, and how strong is
    your
yearning for your children lost between that which
they have attained and that which they could not
    obtain.

We clamor and you smile; we flit
but you stay! . . .

. . . Are you a fruit ripened by the sun?
Do you grow from the tree of Absolute
Knowledge, whose roots extend through
Eternity, and whose branches run through the
    Infinite? . . .

From "Merry Autumn"
    PAUL LAURENCE DUNBAR

Don't talk to me of solemn days
In autumn's time of splendor,
Because the sun shows fewer rays,
And these grow slant and slender.

Why, it's the climax of the year—
The highest time of living!—
'Till naturally its bursting cheer
Just melts into thanksgiving.

"Five Kernels of Corn"

BY HEZEKIAH BUTTERWORTH

Twas the year of the famine in Plymouth of old,
The ice and the snow from the thatched roofs had
   rolled.
Through the warm purple skies steered the geese
   o'er the seas,
And the woodpeckers tapped in the clocks of the
   trees;
The boughs on the slopes to the south winds lay
   bare,
And dreaming of summer the buds swelled in air,
The pale Pilgrims welcomed each reddening morn;
There were left for rations but Five Kernels
   of Corn
     Five Kernels of Corn!
     Five Kernels of Corn!
But to Bradford a feast were Five Kernels
   of Corn!

II
"Five Kernels of Corn! Five Kernels of Corn!
Ye people be glad for Five Kernels of Corn!"
So Bradford cried out on bleak Burial Hill.
And the thin women stood in their doors white
   and still.

(continued)

"Lo the Harbor of Plymouth rolls bright in the
   spring.
The maples grow red, and the wood robins sing,
The west wind is blowing, and fading the snow,
And the pleasant pines sing, and arbutuses blow.
      Five Kernels of Corn!
      Five Kernels of Corn!
To each one be given Five Kernels of Corn!"

III

O Bradford of Austerfield, haste on thy way,
The west winds are blowing o'er Province-town
   Bay,
The white avens bloom, but the pines domes are
   chill,
And new graves have furrowed Precisioners' Hill!
"Give thanks all ye people, the warm skies have
   come,
The hilltops are sunny, and green grows the holm,
And the trumpets of winds, and the white March
   is gone,
And ye still have left you Five Kernels of Corn.
      Five Kernels of Corn!
      Five Kernels of Corn!
Ye have for Thanksgiving Five Kernels of Corn!"

Songs, Hymns, and Anthems

Though central to Thanksgiving, eating wasn't the only activity. Singing, too, had a place. When the Pilgrims arrived in the New World, they had with them a psalter, prepared by biblical scholar Henry Ainsworth. The psalter offered 39 melodies for the 150 psalms Ainsworth selected to suit the Pilgrims' Puritan beliefs.

The Thanksgiving Ceremony concludes with the singing of the most popular verse of "America the Beautiful," before the meal. Liven your festivities—before, during, and after the Ceremony—with the following traditional and contemporary songs and hymns, chosen for the spirit of thanks and patriotic heritage.

Count Your Blessings
BY JOHNSON OATMAN, JR.

Are you ever burdened with a load of care?
Does the cross seem heavy you are called
on to bear?
Count your many blessings, every doubt will fly,
And you will keep singing as the days go by.

Come, Ye Thankful People Come

108

Come ye thankful people come,
Raise the song of harvest home!
All is safely gathered in,
Ere the winter storms begin;
God our Maker, doth provide
For our wants to be supplied:
Come to God's own temple, come,
Raise the song of harvest home.

All the world is God's own field
Fruit unto his praise to yield;
Wheat and tares together sown
Unto joy or sorrow grown;
First the blade, and then the ear,
Then the full corn shall appear;
Lord of the harvest! grant that we
Wholesome grain and pure may be.

For the Lord our God shall come,
And shall take his harvest home;
From his field shall in that day
All offenses purge away,
Give his angels charge at last
In the fire the tares to cast;
But the fruitful ears to store
In his garner evermore.

(continued)

(continued)

Even so, Lord, quickly come,
Bring thy final harvest home;
Gather thou thy people in,
Free from sorrow, free from sin,
There, forever purified,
in thy presence to abide;
Come, with all thine angels, come,
Raise the glorious harvest home.

This Land Is Your Land

BY WOODY GUTHRIE

This land is your land, This land is my land,
From California to the New York island,
From the redwood forest, to the Gulf Stream
    waters:
This land was made for you and me.

As I was walking that ribbon of highway,
I saw above me that endless skyway:
I saw below me that golden valley:
This land was made for you and me.

(continued)

I've roamed and rambled and I followed
   my footsteps
To the sparkling sands of her diamond deserts;
And all around me a voice was sounding:
This land was made for you and me.

When the sun came shining, and I was strolling,
And the wheat fields waving and the dust
   clouds rolling,
As the fog was lifting a voice was chanting:
This land was made for you and me.

As I went walking, I saw a sign there,
And on the sign it said "No Trespassing."
But on the other side it didn't say nothing,
That side was made for you and me.

In the shadow of the steeple I saw my people,
By the relief office I seen my people;
As they stood there hungry, I stood there asking
Is this land made for you and me?

Nobody living can ever stop me,
As I go walking that freedom highway;
Nobody living can make me turn back,
This land was made for you and me.

Thanksgiving Day

BY LYDIA MARIA CHILD

Over the river, and through the wood,
To grandfather's house we go;
The horse knows the way,
To carry the sleigh,
Through the white and drifted snow.

Over the river, and through the wood—
Oh, how the wind does blow!
It stings the toes,
And bites the nose,
As over the ground we go.

Over the river, and through the wood,
To have a first-rate play.
Hear the bells ring
'Ting-a-ling-ding!'
Hurrah for Thanksgiving Day!

Over the river, and through the wood
Trot fast, my dapple-gray!
Spring over the ground,
Like a hunting-hound!
For this is Thanksgiving Day.

(continued)

Over the river and through the wood,
And straight through the barn-yard gate.
We seem to go
Extremely slow,—
It is so hard to wait!

Over the river, and through the wood—
Now grandmother's cap I spy!
Hurrah for the fun!
Is the pudding done?
Hurrah for the pumpkin-pie!

Shine On Harvest Moon

BY NORA BAYES AND JACK NORWORTH

Shine on, shine on harvest moon
Up in the sky,
I ain't had no lovin'
Since January, February, June or July

Snow time ain't no time to stay
Outdoors and spoon,
So shine on, shine on harvest moon,
For me and my gal.

Amazing Grace

BY JOHN NEWTON

Amazing Grace, how sweet the sound,
That saved a wretch like me.
I once was lost but now am found,
Was blind, but now, I see.

'Twas Grace that taught my heart to fear.
And Grace, my fears relieved.
How precious did that Grace appear,
The hour I first believed.

Through many dangers, toils and snares
I have already come.
'Twas Grace that brought me safe thus far,
And Grace will lead me home.

The Lord has promised good to me,
His word my hope secures.
He will my shield and portion be,
As long as life endures.

Yea, when this flesh and heart shall fail,
And mortal life shall cease,
I shall possess, within the veil,
A life of joy and peace.

(continued)

The Thanksgiving Ceremony

(continued)

When we've been here ten thousand years,
Bright shining as the sun,
We've no less days to sing God's praise
Then when we'd first begun.

Amazing Grace, how sweet the sound,
That saved a wretch like me.
I once was lost but now am found,
Was blind, but now, I see.

America the Beautiful

BY KATHERINE LEE BATES AND SAMUEL A. WARD

O beautiful for spacious skies,
For amber waves of grain,
For purple mountain majesties
Above the fruited plain!

America! America!
God shed His grace on thee,
And crown thy good with brotherhood
From sea to shining sea!

(continued)

(continued)

O beautiful for pilgrim feet
Whose stern impassion'd stress
A thoroughfare for freedom beat
Across the wilderness.

America! America!
God mend thine ev'ry flaw,
Confirm thy soul in self-control
Thy liberty in law.

O beautiful for heroes prov'd
In liberating strife,
Who more than self their country loved,
And mercy more than life.

America! America!
May God thy gold refine
Till all success be nobleness,
And ev'ry grain divine.

O beautiful for patriot dream
That sees beyond the years
Thine alabaster cities gleam
Undimmed by human tears.

(continued)

America! America!
God shed His grace on thee,
And crown thy good with brotherhood
From sea to shining sea.

We Gather Together

We Gather Together
To Ask the Lord's Blessing:
He chastens and hastens His will to make known:
The wicked oppressing now cease from
   distressing.
Sing praises to His Name:
He forgets not His Own.

Beside us, to guide us,
Our God with us joining.
Ordaining, maintaining His kingdom divine;
So from the beginning the fight
we were winning:
Thou Lord, wast at our side,
All glory be Thine.

(continued)

(continued)

We all do extol Thee,
Thou leader triumphant,
And pray that Thou still our Defender wilt be.
Let Thy congregation escape tribulation:
Thy Name be ever praised!
O Lord, make us free!

Bringing in the Sheaves

Sowing in the morning, sowing seeds of kindness,
Sowing in the noontide and the dewy eves;
Waiting for the harvest, and the time of reaping,
We shall come, rejoicing, bringing in the sheaves.

Sowing in the sunshine, sowing in the shadows,
Fearing neither clouds nor winter's chilling
    breeze;
By and by the harvest, and the labor ended,
We shall come, rejoicing, bringing in the sheaves.

(continued)

Going forth weeping, sowing for the Master,
Tho' the loss sustained our spirit often grieves;
When our weeping's over, He will bid
   us welcome,
We shall come, rejoicing, bringing in the sheaves.

Chorus:
Bringing in the sheaves, bringing in the sheaves,
We shall come, rejoicing,
Bringing in the sheaves;
Bringing in the sheaves, bringing in the sheaves,
We shall come, rejoicing, bringing in the sheaves.

MY THANKS AND
ACKNOWLEDGMENTS

 This concept has been "germinating" for twenty-five years. Thus, it has accrued many valued contributors.

My Francophone wife calls Thanksgiving the essence of "*l'hospitalité la plus chaleureuse*." At the dinner table of close friends and relatives—particularly: Rebecca and Peter Blechman, Joyce and Bob Menschel, Helene and Bill Safire, Lydia and Arthur Emil, Lionel and the late Suzanne Pincus and Bob Sind—I would invariably think about the deeper meaning of "Thanksgiving" for our "nation of immigrants."

It wasn't until I stepped back from full-time responsibilities at Warner Bros. that I could devote the personal effort necessary for a comprehensive Thanksgiving book. Meanwhile, it was launched by Ona Murdoch's extensive original research, and then put aside for many years until revised and greatly enhanced by Laura Blum, whose congeniality complemented her considerable skills. Much material, on hold for the future, was researched and assembled by Darragh Worland. Jennie Eisenhower dug for hymns, songs, and historical material, reflecting the background of the modest granddaughter and great-granddaughter of two American presidents.

My Thanks and Acknowledgments

Throughout the long germination, my full-time commitment to Warner Bros. greatly indebted me to both Louise Billington for twenty-three years of running my office and to Charlotte Mulford Marlis for twenty-nine years of running my life. Their tireless dedication made all the difference.

Deepest thanks also go to my editor, Annik LaFarge, for recognizing that a powerful idea, simplified and well polished—by her—could resonate in millions of American homes, even in November, when the book industry is obsessively focused on Christmas. And to Karen Minster for the handsome and elegant design, as well as to Dorothy Reinhardt for the artwork expressing the flavor of the holiday. Virginia Creeden handled the arduous task of permissions, paralleled by my editor's always vigilant shepherd, Dorianne Steele.

Also, appreciation to my longtime close friend—and schoolmate since age seven—Mort Janklow, whose name is now usually preceded by "superagent," for finding the resonant professionals at Crown.

And for his typically eloquent, erudite, and witty Foreword, I am indebted to Bill Safire. Over fifty-five years, we have never stopped debating politics. How wonderful we agree on the values of Thanksgiving—and of true friendship.

Were all of these terrific colleagues assembled around my table this November, would I give thanks!

Throughout my many years, scores of other good friends and relatives have been gracious hosts for weekends, at Thanksgiving, Passover, or meals that had *l'hospitalité la plus chaleureuse*, an especially warm family feeling. Some are no longer with us, and some are no longer couples. But, on memorable occasions, their hospitality offered a strong spirit of family and "thanksgiving"—for our collective good fortune. With my apologies for oversight or careless omission, many thanks for the inspiration of:

Cecile, Philip, and Howard Bleier; Hannah and Sam Pomeranz; Fay and Louis Bleier; Juliette and Henri Palacci; Emilie, Sarah, and Eliakim Palacci; Meno, Lena, Juliette, Deborah, and Alex Palacci; Julia and Harold Pomeranz; Bea and Frank Richter; Ethel, Sam, and Ira Scharfer; Henry Chase and Philip Edward Blechman; Henry Marc Palacci; Esther and Oded Aboodi; Thea and Merv Adelson; Arlene and Alan Alda; Shana Alexander; Paige and Ted Ashley; Lorraine and Julie Barnathan; Mary and Chuck Barris; Bob Batscha; Ruth and Joe Baum; Marilyn Berger and Don Hewitt; Pam Bernstein and George Friedman; Ann and Ken Bialkin; Toby and Irving Bieber; Carol and Frank Biondi; Tom Bishop; Melinda and Alan Blinken; Vera and Donald Blinken; Jackie and Cliff Botway; Paul Brach and Miriam Schapiro; Marie Brenner and Ernie Pomerantz; Lori and Rich Bressler; Nancy and Robert Brown; Ellie Bunin and George Munro; DiDi and Jim Burke; Ann and Larry Buttenwieser; Ina and Bob Caro; Gloria and Ann Cestone; Jerry and Marjorie Chester; Maureen and Marshall Cogan; Annie and Robert Cohen; Hildy Parks and Alex Cohen; Pat Collins and Bill Sarnoff; Diane and John Cooke; Joan Cooney and Pete Peterson; Sue Cott and Lester Wunderman; Bob Craig; Joan and Joe Cullman; Ellie and Ron Delsener; Helen and

My Thanks and Acknowledgments

Chuck Dolan; Cathy Doyle and Dick Ravitch; David and Julie Nixon Eisenhower; Jane and Michael Eisner; Mica and Ahmet Ertegun; Florence and Richard Fabrikant; H.R.H. Princess Firyal; Evan Frankel; Julie and Eric Frankel; Betty Friedan; Ruth and Ron Frieman; Michael Fuchs; Frieda and Roy Furman; Danielle and Dick Gardner; Judy and Les Gelb; Skippy and Manny Gerard; Ilene and Stanley Gold; Barbara Goldsmith; Barbara and Roy Goodman; Mark Goodson; Terri Goodson and Dwight Chapin; Margot and Leonard Gordon; Betty Johnson and Arthus Gray; Eleanor Richter Kramer; Brooke Kroeger and Alex Goren; Susan Solomon and Paul Goldberger; Rob Glaser; Arnie and Milly Glimcher; Barbara and Merrill Grant; Agnes Gund and Daniel Shapiro; Jules Haimovitz; Joan and Mort Hamburg; Kitty Carlisle Hart; Rita and Gus Hauser; Marie Christine and John Heimann; Sherrye Henry; Nizza and John Heyman; Courtney Ross and Anders Holst; Jac Holzman; Susan and David Horowitz; Sy and Phyllis Hopman; Linda and Mort Janklow; Kayce and Peter Jennings; Barbara and Donald Jonas; Holly and Howard Kalmenson; Ann and Donald Kanter; Lena and Gil Kaplan; Karen and Harvey Karp; Frances and Norman Katz; Ellen and Victor Kiam; Fran and Ed Kittredge; Isabol and Ron Konecky; Tom Kuhn; Diane and Mort Lacher; Laura Landro and Rick Salomon; Jennifer and George Lang; Evelyn and Leonard Lauder; JoCarol and Ronald Lauder; Ricky and Ralph Lauren; Dahlia and Larry Leeds; Susan and Jerry Leider; Kay and Warner LeRoy; Barbara and Jerry Levin; Simone and Bill Levitt; Judy Licht and Jerry Della

Femina; Evelyn and Ken Lipper; Loretta and Bob Lifton; Ellen and Arthur Liman; Shirley Lord and Abe Rosenthal; Ninah and Michael Lynne; Hillie and David Mahoney; Anita and Warren Manshel; Ellen and Jim Marcus; Charlotte and Kevin Marlis; Patricia Matson; Denise and Alex McNaughton; Dan Melnick; Ronay and Richard Menschel; Dina Merrill and Ted Hartley; Audrey and Maurice Mesulam; Sandy and Ed Meyer; Wendy and Barry Meyer; Lorne Michaels; Judith Miller and Jason Epstein; Arnon Milchan; Alice and Daniel Morgaine; Hadassah and Tom Morgan; Ellie and George Munroe; Gladys and Bob Nederlander; Susan and Donald Newhouse; Victoria and Si Newhouse; Patricia and President Richard Nixon; Pam and Ed Pantzer; Laura and Dick Parsons; Susan and Alan Patricof; Dotty and Marty Payson; Maxine and Ned Pines; Ed and Carolyn Pomeranz; Jessica Reif and Bob Cohen; Midge and Ham Richardson; Cecile Richter; Lynda Pollack and Charles Richter; Liz Robbins and Doug Johnson; Ann and Stuart Robinowitz; Mary Rockefeller; Anita and Yale Roe; Jill and Marshall Rose; Joanna and Dan Rose; Nancy and Jim Rosenfield; Sarah and Mitchell Rosenthal; Nina Rosenwald; Courtney and Steve Ross; Daryl and Steve Roth; Jane and Reed Rubin; Vera Rubin; Jane and Morley Safer; Ellin and Renny Saltzman; Pam and Bill Sarnoff; Doris and Larry Schechter; Lenore and Steve Scheffer; Lori Schiaffino; Peggy and Henry Schleiff; Judy and Herb Schlosser; Suzie and Herb Schmertz; Miquette and Mort Schrader; Paola and Mickey Schulhof; Mary Ann and Buzz Shaw; Sue and Spencer Sherman; Marciarose

My Thanks and Acknowledgments

124

and Jerry Shestack; Stephanie and Fred Shuman; Sydney and Stanley Shuman; Ruth Lande Shuman; Beverly Sills and Peter Greenough; Toni and Bill Simon; Cathy and Bob Sind; Ann and Joe Slater; Virginia and Alan Slifka; Roger Smith; Diane and Mel Sokolow; Mary and David Solomon; Ruth and Harvey Spear; Kate Capshaw and Steven Spielberg; Joanne and Joe Stein; Bob Stern; Lise Hilboltd and Dick Stolley; Leila and Mickey Straus; Lynne and Mickey Tarnopol; Joan and Bob Tisch; Billie and Larry Tisch; Lynn and Peter Tishman; Claire and Leonard Tow; Jean and Ray Troubh; Patricia and Kurt Unger; Melinda and Bill vanden Heuvel; Lauren and John Veronis; Jill Krementz and Kurt Vonnegut; Svetlana and Herb Wachtel; Barbara Walters; Sandy and Bert Wasserman; Gertrude and Palmer Weber; Evelyn and Bob Wechsler; Nina and Walter Weiner; Myrna and Arthur Weiss; Luanne and Frank Wells; Maureen White and Steve Rattner; Margaret and Tom Whitehead; Lois and Marty Whitman; Anita and Byron Wien; Nancy and Harold Williams; Harold Wit; Peter Wolff; Lois Wyse and Lee Guber; Hassie and Dan Yankelovich; Elizabeth Zimmer; Mort Zuckerman; and, surely, many others—who fed me well, in spirit as well as body.

Again, many thanks.

PERMISSIONS

An intensive effort was made to locate all bona fide rights holders. However, because of the historical nature of some material, not all searches were conclusive. The author is grateful for the following permissions, which could be determined:

The Black Family Pledge copyright © 1986 by Maya Angelou. Reprinted by permission of the Helen Braun Agency, Inc.

"Oh Thou Kind Lord" from *Bahá'í Prayers* 1954, copyright © 2002 by the National Spiritual Assembly of the Bahá'ís of the United States. Reprinted with permission of the publisher, the Bahá'í Publishing Trust, Wilmette, Illinois.

Lyric excerpt from "God Bless America" by Irving Berlin on page 83 copyright © 1938, 1939 by Irving Berlin. Copyright © renewed 1965, 1966 by Irving Berlin. Copyright © Assigned the Trustees of the God Bless America Fund. International Copyright Secured. All Rights Reserved. Reprinted by permission.

"For Our Country" from *The Book of Common Prayer* (1928) of the Episcopal Church, USA.

Permissions

ABOUT THE AUTHOR

For several decades Edward Bleier has been a top executive at Warner Bros. and ABC. He's a member of the Council on Foreign Relations and chairman of the Center for Communication. He lives in New York.